DISCIPLE *of* CHRIST

EDUCATION IN VIRTUE®

Let's Pray Together

Meditating on the Mysteries & Virtues of the Rosary

using *lectio divina*

Published by Lumen Ecclesiae Press
4101 East Joy Road
Ann Arbor, Michigan 48105

Catechism of the Catholic Church quotes taken from the English translation of the *Catechism of the Catholic Church* for the United States of America copyright © 1994, United States Catholic Conference —Liberia Editrice Vaticana. English translation of the *Catechism of the Catholic Church* Modifications from the Edito Typica copyright © 1997, United States Catholic Conference, Inc.—Liberia Editrice Vaticana.

Unless otherwise noted, all Scripture texts in this work are taken from the New American Bible, revised edition © 2010, 1991, 1986, 1970 Confraternity of Christian Doctrine, Washington, D.C. and are used by permission of the copyright owner. All rights reserved. No part of the New American Bible may be reproduced in any form without permission in writing from the copyright owner.

Cover Design: Amy Beers
Book Design Layout: Linda Kelly, Amy Beers
Contributors: Sister Mary Samuel Handwerker, OP, Sister Catherine Thomas Brennan, OP, Sr. Maria Veritas Marks, OP

ISBN: 978-1-7323200-2-4

Table of Contents

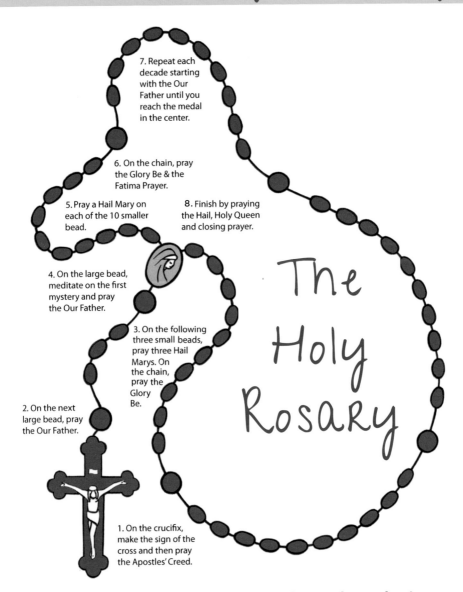

7. Repeat each decade starting with the Our Father until you reach the medal in the center.

6. On the chain, pray the Glory Be & the Fatima Prayer.

5. Pray a Hail Mary on each of the 10 smaller bead.

8. Finish by praying the Hail, Holy Queen and closing prayer.

4. On the large bead, meditate on the first mystery and pray the Our Father.

The Holy Rosary

3. On the following three small beads, pray three Hail Marys. On the chain, pray the Glory Be.

2. On the next large bead, pray the Our Father.

1. On the crucifix, make the sign of the cross and then pray the Apostles' Creed.

Which mysteries to pray (during ordinary time):

Sunday - Glorious Mysteries
Monday - Joyful Mysteries
Tuesday - Sorrowful Mysteries
Wednesday - Glorious Mysteries
Thursday - Luminous Mysteries
Friday - Sorrowful Mysteries
Saturday - Joyful Mysteries

The Sign of the Cross

In the name of the Father, and of the Son, and of the Holy Spirit. Amen.

Apostles' Creed

I believe in God, the Father Almighty, Creator of heaven and earth; and in Jesus Christ, His only Son, our Lord; Who was conceived by the Holy Spirit, born of the Virgin Mary, suffered under Pontius Pilate, was crucified, died, and was buried. He descended into hell; on the third day He arose again from the dead. He ascended into heaven, and sits at the right hand of God, the Father Almighty; from thence He shall come to judge the living and the dead. I believe in the Holy Spirit, the Holy Catholic Church, the communion of Saints, the forgiveness of sins, the resurrection of the body and life everlasting. Amen.

Our Father

Our Father, who art in heaven, hallowed be Thy name; Thy kingdom come; Thy will be done on earth as it is in heaven. Give us this day our daily bread; and forgive us our trespasses as we forgive those who trespass against us; and lead us not into temptation; but deliver us from evil. Amen.

Hail Mary

Hail Mary, full of grace, the Lord is with thee; blessed art thou among women, and blessed is the fruit of thy womb, Jesus. Holy Mary, Mother of God, pray for us sinners, now and at the hour of our death. Amen.

Glory Be

Glory be to the Father, and to the Son, and to the Holy Spirit. As it was in the beginning, is now, and ever shall be, world without end. Amen.

Fatima Prayer

O my Jesus, forgive us our sins, save us from the fires of hell. Lead all souls to Heaven, especially those in most need of Thy mercy.

Hail Holy Queen

Hail, Holy Queen Mother of Mercy, our life, our sweetness and our hope! To thee do we cry, poor banished children of Eve; to thee do we send up our sighs, mourning, and weeping in this vale of tears. Turn then, most gracious advocate, thine eyes of mercy toward us, and after this our exile, show unto us the blessed fruit of thy womb, Jesus. O clement, O loving, O sweet Virgin Mary!

V. Pray for us, O Holy Mother of God.
R. That we may be made worthy of the promises of Christ.

Prayer after the Rosary

Let us pray. O GOD, whose only begotten Son, by His life, death, and resurrection, has purchased for us the rewards of eternal life, grant, we beseech Thee, that meditating upon these mysteries of the Most Holy Rosary of the Blessed Virgin Mary, we may imitate what they contain and obtain what they promise, through the same Christ Our Lord. Amen.

The prayer after the rosary reminds us that by imitating the life, death, and resurrection of Christ, we will obtain eternal happiness with God, Mary, and all the angels and saints in Heaven.

"The goal of the virtuous life is to become like God."
—St. Gregory of Nyssa

To become like God means to live in friendship with Him and participate in His life, which is grace. To live the virtuous life is to look to the person of Jesus Christ and to pursue the habit of doing good.

By praying the rosary and thinking about the life of Christ, one is able to walk with Mary and live joyfully as a disciple.

The practice of all of the virtues is animated and inspired by charity, which "binds everything together in perfect harmony."
—Colossians 3:14, CCC, 1827

"God gives the growth." (1 Corinthians 3:7)

Virtue Chart

VIRTUES	MEANING	OPPOSING TRAIT	WAYS TO CULTIVATE
Justice	Enables one to give to each, beginning with God, what is due him.	Failing to see what is owed to each by virtue of his dignity	Recognize what is due to God first and then to others.
Generosity	Giving of oneself in a willing and cheerful manner for the good of others	Giving without a spirit of cheer, with a begrudging manner	Be self-giving; focus on one act of charity/kindness each day; share.
Gratitude	Thankful disposition of mind and heart	Not expressing appreciation; taking other people and things for granted	Count the good things (blessings) in one's life; express gratitude even when it is difficult.
Loyalty	Accepting the bonds implicit in relationships and defending the virtues upheld by Church, family, and country	Breaking bonds of trust with Church, family, country, friends, and school	Seek to do one's best to help others; follow rules; fulfill responsibilities; be faithful to commitments.
Obedience	Assenting to rightful authority without hesitation or resistance	Resisting the directives of rightful authority	Seek to do one's best to help others; follow rules; fulfill responsibilities; be faithful to commitments.
Prayerfulness	Being still, listening, and being willing to talk to God as a friend	Entertaining distractions during prayers and Mass	Cultivate a spirit of prayer and recollection; maintain the proper posture (kneeling, sitting still, etc.).
Responsibility	Fulfilling one's just duties; accepting the consequences of one's words and actions, intentional and unintentional	Failing to accept responsibility for one's words and/or actions; being unreliable	Be accountable for one's personal actions and decisions at home, at school, and in personal relationships.

VIRTUES	MEANING	OPPOSING TRAIT	WAYS TO CULTIVATE
Prudence (Sound Judgment)	Enables one to reason and to act rightly in any given situation—"right reason in action"	Being hasty or rash in one's words or actions	Pray for guidance. Seek sound advice. Think about the situation. Act upon the decision.
Docility	Willingness to be taught	Being stubborn, inflexible, and proudly set in one's ways	Listen to others and be willing to follow directions; thank others for rightful corrections.

VIRTUES	MEANING	OPPOSING TRAIT	WAYS TO CULTIVATE
Fortitude (Courage)	Enables one to endure difficulties and pain for the sake of what is good	Choosing the easiest task; being cowardly; being insensible to fear	Withstand difficulties; complete hard tasks.
Magnanimity	Seeking with confidence to do great things in God; literally "having a large soul"	Giving in to a lack of motivation to complete one's responsibilities; being lazy	Acknowledge the good in others when it is difficult; strive to do difficult tasks with God's grace.
Patience	Bearing present difficulties calmly	Being impatient while completing a difficult task or in handling challenging circumstances	Listen to others; wait for one's turn; tolerate inconveniences and annoyances without complaining.
Perseverance	Taking the steps necessary to carry out objectives in spite of difficulties	Quickly giving up when a task is challenging	Complete task from start to finish; stay with a task when it is hard, difficult, or boring.

VIRTUES	MEANING	OPPOSING TRAIT	WAYS TO CULTIVATE
Temperance (Self-Control)	Enables one to be moderate in the pleasure and use of created goods	Intemperance; overindulging in a good thing	Exercise the freedom to say 'no' to one's wants and desires.
Honesty	Sincerity, openness, and truthfulness in one's words and actions	Being dishonest in words and actions; telling lies	Live uprightly in words and actions; recognize that "God sees the heart"
Humility	Awareness that all one's gifts come from God and appreciation for the gifts of others	Failing to recognize the gifts of others; being too proud or having false humility	Show deference to others; acknowledge the accomplishments of others; look at one's strengths and weaknesses honestly
Meekness	Serenity of spirit while focusing on the needs of others	Giving in to anger and losing one's temper when working or playing with others	Remain calm; allow others to go first; wait without complaining

Pearl of Wisdom on the Rosary

"Without thinking of what I was doing I took my Rosary in my hands and went on my knees. The Lady made with Her head a sign of approval and Herself took into Her hands a Rosary which hung on Her right arm… The Lady left me to pray all alone; She passed the beads of Her Rosary between Her fingers but She said nothing; only at the end of each decade did She say the 'Gloria' with me."

—St. Bernadette of Soubirous, describing the first apparition of Our Lady at Lourdes

the Joyful Mysteries

1. **The Annunciation**
2. **The Visitation**
3. **The Nativity**
4. **The Presentation**
5. **The Finding of Jesus in the Temple**

The first five decades, the "joyful mysteries," are marked by *the joy radiating from the event of the Incarnation*...The whole of humanity, in turn, is embraced by the fiat with which [Mary] readily agrees to the will of God...To meditate upon the "joyful" mysteries, then, is to enter into the ultimate causes and the deepest meaning of Christian joy. Mary leads us to discover the secret of Christian joy, reminding us that Christianity is, first and foremost, *evangelion*, "good news," which has as its heart and its whole content the person of Jesus Christ, the Word made flesh, the one Saviour of the world.

St. Pope John Paul II, *Rosarium Virginis Mariae* n. 20

1. THE ANNUNCIATION
(Luke 1:26-38, John 1:14)

I'M PRAYING THIS DECADE FOR: _____

- God sends the Archangel Gabriel to Nazareth.
- The Angel greets Mary: "Hail, full of grace; the Lord is with thee" (Luke 1:28) and tells her that she is to be the Mother of God.
- Mary consents: "Behold I am the handmaid of the Lord; be it done unto me according to thy word." (Luke 1:38)
- God becomes man: the Word is made flesh.

In the sixth month, the angel Gabriel was sent from God to a town of Galilee called Nazareth, to a virgin betrothed to a man named Joseph, of the house of David, and the virgin's name was Mary. And coming to her, he said, "Hail, favored one! The Lord is with you." But she was greatly troubled at what was said and pondered what sort of greeting this might be. Then the angel said to her, "Do not be afraid, Mary, for you have found favor with God. Behold, you will conceive in your womb and bear a son, and you shall name him Jesus. He will be great and will be called Son of the Most High, and the Lord God will give him the throne of David his father, and he will rule over the house of Jacob forever, and of his kingdom there will be no end." But Mary said to the angel, "How can this be, since I have no relations with a man?" And the angel said to her in reply, "The holy Spirit will come upon you, and the power of the Most High will overshadow you. Therefore the child to be born will be called holy, the Son of God. And behold, Elizabeth, your relative, has also conceived a son in her old age, and this is the sixth month for her who was called barren; for nothing will be impossible for God." Mary said, "Behold, I am the handmaid of the Lord. May it be done to me according to your word." Then the angel departed from her.

Lectio Divina | PRAYING WITH SCRIPTURE

Ask this question in prayer: "Jesus my God, You showed great humility by becoming a child in the womb of the Virgin Mary. In what ways do I need to be more humble?" What do you hear Him saying to you?

VIRTUE | HUMILITY

Awareness that all one's gifts come from God and appreciation of the gifts of others

Ways to Cultivate This Virtue

- Recognize the gifts and talents of others and compliment them.
- Give other people credit.
- Go last.
- Spend more time listening to others.
- Thank God for His gifts to you.

13

I'M PRAYING THIS DECADE FOR: _____

- Mary hastens to visit her elderly cousin Elizabeth in her time of need.
- When Mary greets Elizabeth, John hears Mary's voice and leaps for joy in his mother's womb.
- Elizabeth praises Mary: "Blessed art thou among women, and blessed is the fruit of thy womb." (Luke 1:42)
- Mary returns praise to God: "My soul magnifies the Lord." (Luke 1:46)
- Mary helps Elizabeth for three months until she gives birth to John the Baptist.

During those days Mary set out and traveled to the hill country in haste to a town of Judah, where she entered the house of Zechariah and greeted Elizabeth. When Elizabeth heard Mary's greeting, the infant in her womb leaped in her womb, and Elizabeth, filled with the Holy Spirit, cried out in a loud voice and said, "Most blessed are you among women, and blessed is the fruit of your womb. And how does this happen to me, that the mother of my Lord should come to me? For at the moment the sound of your greeting reached my ears, the infant in my womb leaped for joy. Blessed are you who believed that what was spoken to you by the Lord would be fulfilled."

And Mary said:
"My soul proclaims the greatness of the Lord;
    my spirit rejoices in God my savior.
For he has looked upon his handmaid's lowliness;
    behold, from now on will all ages call me blessed.
The Mighty One has done great things for me,
    and holy is his name…"

Mary remained with her about three months and then returned to her home.

Lectio Divina | PRAYING WITH SCRIPTURE

Ask this question in prayer: "Jesus, Your mother Mary cheerfully gave of herself in going quickly to help Elizabeth. How can I be more generous today?" What do you hear Him saying to you?

VIRTUE | GENEROSITY

Giving of oneself in a willing and cheerful manner for the good of others

Ways to Cultivate This Virtue
• Share your items and time.
• Give away extra clothes or items you have.
• Give of yourself; focus on one act of charity or kindness each day.

I'M PRAYING THIS DECADE FOR: _____

- Mary and Joseph travel to Bethlehem.
- Mary and Joseph are turned away from the inn; there is no room for them.
- Joseph finds shelter in a stable.
- Jesus is born, and Mary wraps Him in swaddling clothes and lays Him in a manger.
- Mary ponders these things in her heart.

SCRIPTURE | Luke 2:4–11,15–19

And Joseph too went up from Galilee from the town of Nazareth to Judea, to the city of David that is called Bethlehem, because he was of the house and family of David, to be enrolled with Mary, his betrothed, who was with child. While they were there, the time came for her to have her child, and she gave birth to her firstborn son. She wrapped him in swaddling clothes and laid him in a manger, because there was no room for them in the inn.

Now there were shepherds in that region living in the fields and keeping the night watch over their flock. The angel of the Lord appeared to them and the glory of the Lord shone around them, and they were struck with great fear. The angel said to them, "Do not be afraid; for behold, I proclaim to you good news of great joy that will be for all the people. For today in the city of David a savior has been born for you who is Messiah and Lord."

…When the angels went away from them to heaven, the shepherds said to one another, "Let us go, then, to Bethlehem to see this thing that has taken place, which the Lord has made known to us." So they went in haste and found Mary and Joseph, and the infant lying in the manger. When they saw this, they made known the message that had been told them about this child. All who heard it were amazed… And Mary kept all these things, reflecting on them in her heart.

Lectio Divina | PRAYING WITH SCRIPTURE

Ask this question in prayer: "Jesus, You were born in a stable because there was no room in the inn. How can I open my heart to welcome You today?" What do you hear Him saying to you?

VIRTUE | TEMPERANCE

Enables one to be moderate in the pleasure and use of created goods.

Ways to Cultivate This Virtue

- Freely say "no" to something you want.
- Be moderate in your possessions, i.e., toys, clothes.
- Take only one snack or dessert.

I'M PRAYING THIS DECADE FOR: _____

- Mary and Joseph bring the Infant Jesus to the Temple.
- The elderly Simeon sees the Christ Child and recognizes Him as the Messiah.
- Simeon receives the Christ Child into his arms.
- Simeon blesses Mary and Joseph and foretells the destiny of the Child and the sorrows of His Mother.
- Anna, who leads a life of prayer and penance in the Temple, also recognizes the Savior and speaks of Him to the people.

SCRIPTURE | Luke 2:22–38

When the days were completed for their purification according to the law of Moses, they took him up to Jerusalem to present him to the Lord, just as it is written in the law of the Lord. Now there was a man in Jerusalem whose name was Simeon. This man was righteous and devout, awaiting the consolation of Israel, and the holy Spirit was upon him. He came in the Spirit into the temple; and when the parents brought in the child Jesus to perform the custom of the law in regard to him, he took him into his arms and blessed God. The child's father and mother were amazed at what was said about him; and Simeon blessed them and said to Mary his mother, "Behold, this child is destined for the fall and rise of many in Israel, and to be a sign that will be contradicted (and you yourself a sword will pierce) so that the thoughts of many hearts may be revealed."

There was also a prophetess, Anna, the daughter of Phanuel, of the tribe of Asher. She was advanced in years, having lived with her husband after her marriage, and then as a widow until she was eighty-four. She never left the temple, but worshiped night and day with fasting and prayer. And coming forward at that very time, she gave thanks to God and spoke about the child to all who were awaiting the redemption of Jerusalem.

Lectio Divina | PRAYING WITH SCRIPTURE

Ask this question in prayer: "Jesus, Joseph and Mary presented You in the temple to fulfill the law and to dedicate You to God. This was an act of love and obedience. Teach me how to hear and obey You." What do you hear Him saying to you?

VIRTUE | OBEDIENCE

Assenting to rightful authority without hesitation or resistance

Ways to Cultivate This Virtue
- Follow God's commandments.
- Listen and follow directions the first time without complaint.
- Listen to your teachers, parents, babysitters, etc.

I'M PRAYING THIS DECADE FOR: _____

- When Jesus is twelve, He and Mary and Joseph go to Jerusalem to celebrate the feast of Passover, as they do every year.

- After the feast, Mary and Joseph leave Jerusalem, but Jesus remains behind without His parents knowing.

- Realizing Jesus is missing, Mary and Joseph search for Him for three days.

- Mary and Joseph find Jesus in the Temple in the midst of the teachers.

- Mary receives her Child in joy and anguish, and Jesus explains that He was doing His Father's work.

SCRIPTURE | Luke 2:41–51

Each year his parents went to Jerusalem for the feast of Passover, and when he was twelve years old, they went up according to festival custom. After they had completed its days, as they were returning, the boy Jesus remained behind in Jerusalem, but his parents did not know it. Thinking that he was in the caravan, they journeyed for a day and looked for him among their relatives and acquaintances, but not finding him, they returned to Jerusalem to look for him. After three days they found him in the temple, sitting in the midst of the teachers, listening to them and asking them questions, and all who heard him were astounded at his understanding and his answers. When his parents saw him, they were astonished, and his mother said to him, "Son, why have you done this to us? Your father and I have been looking for you with great anxiety." And he said to them, "Why were you looking for me? Did you not know that I must be in my Father's house?" But they did not understand what he said to them. He went down with them and came to Nazareth, and was obedient to them; and his mother kept all these things in her heart.

Lectio Divina | PRAYING WITH SCRIPTURE

Ask this question in prayer: "Jesus, in remaining in Your Father's house, You teach us to keep God first in our lives. In returning to Nazareth with Mary and Joseph, You teach us to obey our parents and rightful authorities. How can I put God first in my life today?" What do you hear Him saying to you?

VIRTUE | JUSTICE

Enables one to give to each, beginning with God, what is due him

Ways to Cultivate This Virtue

- Always tell the truth, even when it is difficult.
- Practice speaking, thinking, and acting kindly.
- Give more time praying to God.
- Pay attention to whomever you are speaking with, either God or others.

Pearls of Wisdom on the Rosary

"Of all our prayers to the Mother of Mercy, the one which the Church urges us most insistently [to pray] is the rosary, the recital of which God rewards with countless graces and blessings."

—Blessed Michael Sopocko

"Love the Madonna and pray the rosary, for her rosary is the weapon against the evils of the world today."

—St. Padre Pio

the Luminous Mysteries

1. **The Baptism in the Jordan**
2. **The Wedding at Cana**
3. **The Proclamation of the Kingdom**
4. **The Transfiguration**
5. **The Institution of the Eucharist**

Certainly the whole mystery of Christ is a mystery of light. He is the "light of the world" (John 8:12). Yet this truth emerges in a special way during the years of his public life, when he proclaims the Gospel of the Kingdom...Each of these mysteries is *a revelation of the Kingdom now present in the very person of Jesus.* In these mysteries, apart from the miracle at Cana, *the presence of Mary remains in the background*...Yet the role she assumed at Cana in some way accompanies Christ throughout his ministry...the great maternal counsel which Mary addresses to the Church of every age and to us: "Do whatever he tells you" (John 2:5).

St. John Paul II, *Rosarium Virginis Mariae* n. 21

I'M PRAYING THIS DECADE FOR: _____

- John the Baptist preaches repentance in the desert of Judea.
- John baptizes many people in the Jordan River.
- Jesus asks John to baptize Him.
- As Jesus comes up from the water, the heavens are opened, a dove descends, and a voice says, "This is my beloved Son, with whom I am well pleased." (Matthew 3:17)

In those days John the Baptist appeared, preaching in the desert of Judea [and] saying, "Repent, for the kingdom of heaven is at hand!" At that time Jerusalem, all Judea, and the whole region around the Jordan were going out to him and were being baptized by him in the Jordan River as they acknowledged their sins. Then Jesus came from Galilee to John at the Jordan to be baptized by him. John tried to prevent him, saying, "I need to be baptized by you, and yet you are coming to me?" Jesus said to him in reply, "Allow it now, for thus it is fitting for us to fulfill all righteousness." Then he allowed him. After Jesus was baptized, he came up from the water and behold, the heavens were opened for him, and he saw the Spirit of God descending like a dove and coming upon him. And a voice came from the heavens, saying, "This is my beloved Son, with whom I am well pleased."

Lectio Divina | PRAYING WITH SCRIPTURE

Ask this question in prayer: "Jesus, by the grace of baptism, I have become an adopted child of God, cleansed from sin and given the virtues and gifts of the Holy Spirit. How can I better live as a child of God." What do you hear Him saying to you?

VIRTUE | RESPONSIBILITY

Fulfilling our just duties; accepting the consequences of one's words and actions, intentional and unintentional

Ways to Cultivate This Virtue

- Complete your tasks in a timely manner.
- Admit when you are wrong or have done something wrong.
- Be accountable for decisions and actions.

I'M PRAYING THIS DECADE FOR: _____

- A couple is getting married and invite Mary; Jesus and His disciples also come.
- Mary notices that the wine has run out and informs Jesus.
- Mary instructs the waiters to do whatever Jesus tells them to do.
- Jesus changes a great amount of water into wine.
- Jesus' disciples begin to believe in Him.

There was a wedding at Cana in Galilee and the mother of Jesus was there. Jesus and his disciples were also invited to the wedding. When the wine ran short, the mother of Jesus said to him, "They have no wine." And Jesus said to her, "Woman, how does your concern affect me? My hour has not yet come." His mother said to the servers, "Do whatever he tells you." Now there were six stone water jars there, each holding twenty to thirty gallons. Jesus told them, "Fill the jars with water." So they filled them to the brim. Then he told them, "Draw some out now and take it to the headwaiter." So they took it. And when the headwaiter tasted the water that had become wine, without knowing where it came from (although the servers who had drawn the water knew), the head-waiter called the bridegroom and said to him, "Everyone serves good wine first, and then when people have drunk freely, an inferior one; but you have kept the good wine until now." Jesus did this as the beginning of his signs in Cana in Galilee and so revealed his glory, and his disciples began to believe in him.

Lectio Divina | PRAYING WITH SCRIPTURE

Ask this question in prayer: "Jesus, Mary asked You to perform Your first miracle by telling the servants to 'do whatever He tells you.' What am I supposed to learn from Mary in this passage?" What do you hear Him saying to you?

VIRTUE | DOCILITY

Willingness to be taught

Ways to Cultivate This Virtue

- Follow directions; be willing to take turns.
- Listen to your teacher, parents, babysitter.
- Thank others for rightful corrections.

I'M PRAYING THIS DECADE FOR: _____

- Jesus calls us to be converted and to believe in the gospel.
- Jesus heals the sick, forgives sins, comforts the sorrowful, and expels the evil spirits.
- Jesus instructs the crowd on the Sermon on the Mount.
- Jesus proclaims, "The kingdom of God is at hand." (Mark 1:15)

When he saw the crowds, he went up the mountain, and after he had sat down, his disciples came to him. He began to teach them, saying:

"Blessed are the poor in spirit,
  for theirs is the kingdom of heaven.
Blessed are they who mourn,
  for they will be comforted.
Blessed are the meek,
  for they will inherit the land.
Blessed are they who hunger and thirst for righteousness,
  for they will be satisfied.
Blessed are the merciful,
  for they will be shown mercy.
Blessed are the clean of heart,
  for they will see God.
Blessed are the peacemakers,
  for they will be called children of God.
Blessed are they who are persecuted for the sake of righteousness,
  for theirs is the kingdom of heaven.
Blessed are you when they insult you and persecute you and utter every kind of evil against you [falsely] because of me. Rejoice and be glad, for your reward will be great in heaven."

Lectio Divina | PRAYING WITH SCRIPTURE

As you pray this decade, imagine being present on the mountain listening to Jesus. Ask this question in prayer: "Jesus, which beatitude do I need to live?" What do you hear Him saying to you?"

VIRTUE | HONESTY

Sincerity, openness, and truthfulness in one's words and actions

Ways to Cultivate This Virtue

- Tell the truth even if it means you will get in trouble.
- Don't cover up your mistakes when people point them out to you.
- Be aware that God knows your heart.
- Don't hide things from your parents or friends.

I'M PRAYING THIS DECADE FOR: _____

- Jesus takes Peter, James, and John up a mountain.
- On the mountain, Jesus is transfigured: His face shines like the sun and His clothes become brilliantly white.
- Jesus speaks with Moses and Elijah.
- A bright cloud overshadows Jesus and the Apostles.
- From the cloud, a voice says, "This is my beloved Son; listen to Him." (Matthew 17:5)

Jesus took Peter, James and John and led them up a high mountain set apart by themselves. And he was transfigured before them; his face shone like the sun and his clothes became white as light. Then Elijah appeared to them along with Moses, and they were conversing with Jesus.

While he was still speaking, behold, a bright cloud came, casting a shadow over them; then from the cloud came a voice, "This is my beloved Son, with whom I am well pleased. Listen to him." When the disciples heard this, they fell prostrate and were very much afraid. But Jesus came and touched them, saying, "Rise, and do not be afraid." And when the disciples raised their eyes, they saw no one else but Jesus alone.

Lectio Divina | PRAYING WITH SCRIPTURE

Ask this question in prayer: "Jesus, Your Father tells us to listen to You. Show me how I can better listen and think before acting." What do you hear Him saying to you?

VIRTUE | PRUDENCE

Enables one to reason and to act rightly in any given situation —"right reason in action."

Ways to Cultivate This Virtue
- Ask advice from trustworthy people.
- Carefully think about a decision.
- Pray about what the Lord would have you do.
- Ask and listen, think, act.

I'M PRAYING THIS DECADE FOR: _____

- Jesus gathers His Apostles in the Upper Room to celebrate Passover.
- Jesus washes the Apostles' feet and gives them a new commandment, to love one another.
- Jesus changes bread into His Body and wine into His Blood.
- Jesus commands the Apostles to do this in His memory.

When the hour came, Jesus took his place at table with the apostles. He said to them, "I have eagerly desired to eat this Passover with you before I suffer, for, I tell you, I shall not eat it [again] until there is fulfillment in the kingdom of God." Then he took the bread, said the blessing, broke it, and gave it to them, saying, "This is my body, which will be given for you; do this in memory of me." And likewise the cup after they had eaten, saying, "This cup is the new covenant in my blood, which will be shed for you. And yet behold, the hand of the one who is to betray me is with me on the table; for the Son of Man indeed goes as it has been determined; but woe to that man by whom he is betrayed." And they began to debate among themselves who among them would do such a deed.

Lectio Divina | PRAYING WITH SCRIPTURE

Ask this question in prayer: "Jesus, You give Your body, blood, soul, and divinity to us at every Holy Mass. Teach me how to receive You and love You in each Holy Communion." What do you hear Him saying to you?

VIRTUE | GRATITUDE

Thankful disposition of mind and heart

Ways to Cultivate This Virtue

- Smile at your mom or dad and thank them after they cooks dinner.
- Write a thank you note to someone who has given you something.
- Thank God for the blessings in your life.
- Compliment someone.

Pearls of Wisdom on the Rosary

"The rosary can bring families through all dangers and evils."
—Servant of God Patrick Peyton

"In the rosary, we not only say prayers; we think them."
—Venerable Fulton J. Sheen

"The great remedy of modern times, which will influence the events of the world more than all diplomatic endeavors and which has a greater effect on public life than all organizational ones, is the rosary."
—Servant of God Joseph Kentenich

the Sorrowful Mysteries

1. **The Agony in the Garden**
2. **The Scourging at the Pillar**
3. **The Crowning with Thorns**
4. **Jesus Carries the Cross**
5. **The Crucifixion of Our Lord**

The rosary selects certain moments from the Passion, inviting the faithful to contemplate them in their hearts and to relive them...This abject suffering reveals not only the love of God but also the meaning of man himself. *Ecce homo*: the meaning, origin and fulfillment of man is to be found in Christ, the God who humbles himself out of love "even unto death, death on a cross" (Phil. 2:8). The sorrowful mysteries help the believer to relive the death of Jesus, to stand at the foot of the Cross beside Mary, to enter with her into the depths of God's love for man, and to experience all its life-giving power.

St. John Paul II, *Rosarium Virginis Mariae* n. 22

I'M PRAYING THIS DECADE FOR: _____

- After the Last Supper, Jesus and the Apostles go to the Garden of Olives.
- Jesus asks the Apostles to watch with Him, then withdraws to pray.
- As Jesus prays, He is bathed in a sweat of blood; He asks His Father that He not have to drink the chalice of suffering.
- Jesus returns to His Apostles and finds them asleep.
- Jesus goes to meet Judas, His betrayer. His Apostles flee.

Then Jesus came with them to a place called Gethsemane, and he said to his disciples, "Sit here while I go over there and pray." He took along Peter and the two sons of Zebedee, and began to feel sorrow and distress. Then he said to them, "My soul is sorrowful even unto death. Remain here and keep watch with me." He advanced a little and fell prostrate in prayer, saying, "My Father, if it is possible, let this cup pass from me; yet, not as I will, but as you will." When he returned to his disciples he found them asleep. He said to Peter, "So you could not keep watch with me for one hour? Watch and pray that you may not undergo the test. The spirit is willing, but the flesh is weak." Withdrawing a second time, he prayed again, "My Father, if it is not possible that this cup pass without my drinking it, your will be done!" Then he returned once more and found them asleep, for they could not keep their eyes open. He left them and withdrew a third time, saying the same thing again. Then he returned to his disciples and said to them, "Are you still sleeping and taking your rest? Behold, the hour is at hand when the Son of Man is to be handed over to sinners. Get up, let us go. Look, my betrayer is at hand."

Lectio Divina | PRAYING WITH SCRIPTURE

Ask this question in prayer: "Jesus, in the garden You prayed alone and spoke to Your Father. Show me how to spend time alone, talking to the Father." What do you hear Him saying to you?

VIRTUE | PRAYERFULNESS

Being still, listening, and being willing to talk to God as a friend

Ways to Cultivate This Virtue
- Pay attention to the words you say when you pray.
- Be still and listen to what God says to you.
- Fold your hands while you pray.
- Make visits to the chapel.
- Create a place of prayer in your home.

I'M PRAYING THIS DECADE FOR: _____

- The people cry for Christ's crucifixion.
- Pilate orders Jesus to be scourged even though He is innocent.
- Jesus is stripped of His clothes and bound to the pillar.
- He is whipped by the soldiers.
- Jesus suffers meekly.

But he was pierced for our offenses,
> crushed for our sins…
Upon him was the chastisement that makes us whole,
> By his stripes we were healed…
And he shall take away the sins of many, and win pardon for their offenses. (Isaiah 53:2–5, 12)

Pilate, wishing to satisfy the crowd, released Barabbas to them and, after he had Jesus scourged, handed him over to be crucified. (Mark 15:15)

Then Pilate took Jesus and had him scourged. (John 19:1)

Lectio Divina | PRAYING WITH SCRIPTURE

Ask this question in prayer: "Jesus, when they stripped off Your clothes and beat You, You did not complain. What sacrifice can I offer for You with a smile instead of complaining today?" What do you hear Him saying to you?

VIRTUE | MEEKNESS

Serenity of spirit while focusing on the needs of others

Ways to Cultivate This Virtue

- When you get upset, count to ten before you react.
- Walk away when you are angry instead of fighting.
- Allow others to go first; remain calm and wait patiently.

3. THE CROWNING WITH THORNS
(Matthew 27:29–30, Mark 15:16-20, John 19:2–3)

I'M PRAYING THIS DECADE FOR: _____

- The soldiers surround Christ, clothe Him in royal purple, and mock Him.
- They weave a crown out of thorns and place it on His head.
- The soldiers place a reed in Jesus' hand, spit upon Him, and strike His face.
- He endures with fortitude.

Even as many were amazed at him—
so marred were his features,
beyond that of mortals
his appearance, beyond that of human beings —

So shall he startle many nations,
kings shall stand speechless;
For those who have not been told shall see,
those who have not heard shall ponder it. (Isaiah 52:14–15)

Then the soldiers of the governor took Jesus inside the praetorium and gathered the whole cohort around him. They stripped off his clothes and threw a scarlet military cloak about him. Weaving a crown out of thorns, they placed it on his head, and a reed in his right hand. And kneeling before him, they mocked him saying, "Hail, King of the Jews!" They spat upon him and took the reed and kept striking him on the head. (Matthew 27:27–30)

So Jesus came out, wearing the crown of thorns and the purple cloak. And Pilate said to them, "Behold, the man!" (John 19:5)

Lectio Divina | PRAYING WITH SCRIPTURE

Ask this question in prayer: "Jesus, when the soldiers mocked You, no one stood up to defend You. Show me how You want me to be courageous and stand up for someone who needs me." What do you hear Him saying to you?

VIRTUE | FORTITUDE (COURAGE)

Enables one to endure difficulties and pain for the sake of what is good

Ways to Cultivate This Virtue

- Don't give up when things are difficult.
- Do the right thing even when it is hard to do.
- Finish your jobs in a timely manner.
- Don't engage in gossip or unkind talk.

I'M PRAYING THIS DECADE FOR: _____

- Pilate condemns Jesus to death.
- Jesus takes up His cross and carries it toward Mount Calvary.
- The people jeer at Christ.
- Simon of Cyrene is forced to help carry the cross, because Jesus is so weak from the scourging.
- Jesus speaks to the women who are weeping along His path.

When Pilate saw that he was not succeeding at all, but that a riot was breaking out instead, he took water and washed his hands in the sight of the crowd, saying, "I am innocent of this man's blood. Look to it yourselves." And the whole people said in reply, "His blood be upon us and upon our children." Then he released Barabbas to them, but after he had Jesus scourged, he handed him over to be crucified.

And when they had mocked him, they stripped him of the cloak, dressed him in his own clothes and led him off to crucify him. As they were going out, they met a Cyrenian named Simon; this man they pressed into service to carry his cross.

Lectio Divina | PRAYING WITH SCRIPTURE

Ask this question in prayer: "Jesus, when we patiently accept difficulties and not getting our own way, we, too, take up our cross to follow You. Show me how to have patience with my family or friends today and with the difficulties in my life." What do you hear Him saying to you?

VIRTUE | PATIENCE

Bearing present difficulties calmly

Ways to Cultivate This Virtue

- Try to notice when you are responding with impatience.
- Do not get upset if things do not go your way.
- Be a good listener and don't interrupt; wait your turn.

I'M PRAYING THIS DECADE FOR: _____

- Jesus is stripped of His garments and nailed to the cross.

- The people mock Jesus.

- Jesus asks God the Father to forgive His enemies.

- He asks His Mother to be a mother to John and asks John to take care of His Mother.

- Jesus dies on the cross.

When they came to the place called the Skull, they crucified him and the criminals there, one on his right, the other on his left. Then Jesus said, "Father, forgive them, they know not what they do." (Luke 23:33–34)

Then he said, "Jesus, remember me when you come into your kingdom." He replied to him, "Amen, I say to you, today you will be with me in Paradise." (Luke 23:42–43)

When Jesus saw his mother and the disciple there whom he loved, he said to his mother, "Woman, behold, your son." Then he said to the disciple, "Behold, your mother." And from that hour the disciple took her into his home. (John 19:26–27)

And about three o'clock Jesus cried out in a loud voice, "Eli, Eli, lema sabachthani?" which means, "My God, my God, why have you forsaken me?" (Matthew 27:46)

"It is finished." (John 19:30)

Jesus cried out in a loud voice, "Father, into your hands I commend my spirit"; and when he had said this he breathed his last. (Luke 23:46)

Lectio Divina | PRAYING WITH SCRIPTURE

Ask this question in prayer: "Jesus, You love us so much that You died on the cross so that we could be with You in Heaven. You even prayed for those who were cruel to You. Show me how to persevere in love even when it is difficult and when people are treating me unkindly." What do you hear Him saying to you?

VIRTUE | PERSEVERANCE

Taking the steps necessary to carry out objectives in spite of difficulties

Ways to Cultivate This Virtue

- Finish your chores and homework even when you don't feel like it.
- Stay kneeling at Mass when required.
- Complete a task from start to finish.
- Stay faithful to your daily prayers—your conversation with God.

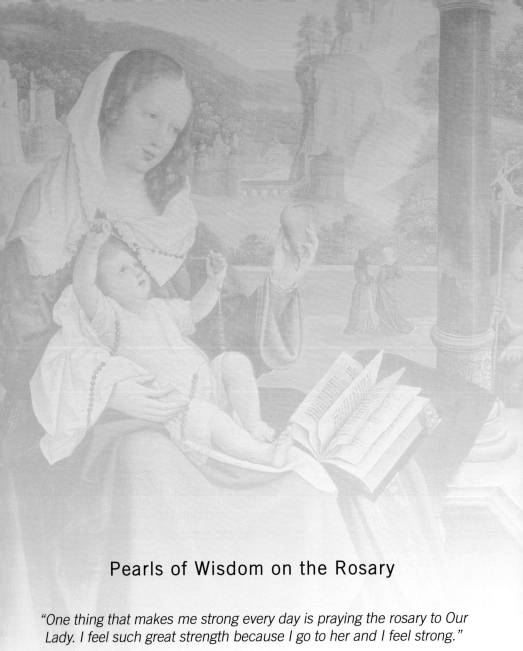

Pearls of Wisdom on the Rosary

"One thing that makes me strong every day is praying the rosary to Our Lady. I feel such great strength because I go to her and I feel strong."

—Pope Francis

"Just as two friends, frequently in each other's company, tend to develop similar habits, so, too, by holding familiar converse with Jesus and the Blessed Virgin, by meditating on the mysteries of the rosary, and by living the same life in Holy Communion, we can become, to the extent of our lowliness, similar to them, and learn from these supreme models a life of humility, poverty, hiddenness, patience, and perfection."

—Blessed Bartolo Longo

the Glorious Mysteries

1. **The Resurrection**
2. **The Ascension**
3. **The Descent of the Holy Spirit**
4. **The Assumption**
5. **The Coronation**

The contemplation of Christ's face cannot stop at the image of the Crucified One. He is the Risen One! The rosary has always...invited the believer to pass beyond the darkness of the Passion in order to gaze upon Christ's glory in the Resurrection and Ascension. Contemplating the Risen One, Christians *rediscover the reasons for their own faith* (cf. 1 Cor. 15:14) and relive the joy not only of those to whom Christ appeared—the Apostles, Mary Magdalene and the disciples on the road to Emmaus—but also the joy of Mary.

St. John Paul II, *Rosarium Virginis Mariae* n. 23

I'M PRAYING THIS DECADE FOR: _____

- Christ rises from the dead.
- At different times, Peter, John, and the women who followed Jesus go to His tomb; they all find it empty, with the burial cloths still inside.
- An angel announces the Resurrection.
- Jesus appears alive to Mary Magdalene and, later, to the Apostles.

After the Sabbath, as the first day of the week was dawning, Mary Magdalene and the other Mary came to the tomb. And behold, there was a great earthquake; for an angel of the Lord descended from heaven, approached, rolled back the stone, and sat upon it. The guards were shaken with fear of him and became like dead men. Then the angel said to the women in reply, "Do not be afraid! I know that you are seeking Jesus the Crucified. He is not here, for he has been raised just as he said. Come and see the place where he lay. Then go quickly and tell his disciples, 'He has been raised from the dead, and he is going before you to Galilee; there you will see him.' Behold, I have told you." Then they went away quickly from the tomb, fearful yet overjoyed, and ran to announce this to his disciples. And behold, Jesus met them on their way and greeted them. They approached, embraced his feet, and did him homage. Then Jesus said to them, "Do not be afraid. Go tell my brothers to go to Galilee, and there they will see me."

Lectio Divina | PRAYING WITH SCRIPTURE

"Jesus, because You rose from the dead, we know that everything You said is true and that You have the power to do anything." Think of something that you are afraid of, and give that to Jesus. What do you hear Him saying to you?

VIRTUE | FAITH

Enables one to know God and all that He has revealed

Ways to Cultivate This Virtue

- Regularly receive the Sacraments: Reconciliation, Holy Communion.
- Read the Bible and tell your friends about Jesus.
- Share your love of God with others.
- Tell God you believe in Him and ask Him to increase your faith.
- Pray an Act of Faith.

I'M PRAYING THIS DECADE FOR: _____

- For forty days after His Resurrection, Jesus spends times with the Apostles and disciples.

- Jesus tells the Apostles to preach the Gospel to the whole world and baptize in the name of the Father, and of the Son, and of the Holy Spirit.

- Jesus commands them to stay in Jerusalem until the Holy Spirit comes.

- Jesus leads the Apostles and disciples out of Jerusalem; in their presence, He ascends into heaven.

- Angels reassure Christ's followers and promise that He will return.

SCRIPTURE | Mark 16:19–20; Luke 24:50–53; Acts 1:9–11

So then the Lord Jesus, after he spoke to them, was taken up into heaven and took his seat at the right hand of God. But they went forth and preached everywhere, while the Lord worked with them and confirmed the word through accompanying signs. (Mark 16:19–20)

Then he led them out as far as Bethany, raised his hands, and blessed them. As he blessed them he parted from them and was taken up to heaven. They did him homage and then returned to Jerusalem with great joy, and they were continually in the temple praising God. (Luke 24:50–53)

When he had said this, as they were looking on, he was lifted up, and a cloud took him from their sight. While they were looking intently at the sky as he was going, suddenly two men dressed in white garments stood beside them. They said, "Men of Galilee, why are you standing there looking at the sky? This Jesus who has been taken up from you into heaven will return in the same way as you have seen him going into heaven. (Acts 1:9–11)

Lectio Divina | PRAYING WITH SCRIPTURE

Ask this question in prayer: "Jesus, You ascended into heaven and left us to be Your witnesses. In what ways can I be a more faithful witness so others may believe in You?" What do you hear Him saying to you?

VIRTUE | HOPE

Enables one to desire God above all things and to trust Him for personal salvation

Ways to Cultivate This Virtue
- Look to the saints in heaven as friends.
- Jesus ascended into heaven. We trust in Him for mercy and forgiveness.
- Live each day desiring to be in heaven.

I'M PRAYING THIS DECADE FOR: _____

- The apostles persevere in prayer with Mary in the Upper Room.
- On Pentecost Sunday, fifty days after the Resurrection, the sound of a mighty wind fills the room, and tongues of fire rest on the apostles.
- The disciples are filled with the Holy Spirit.
- The people are amazed, because each hears the apostles speaking in his own language.
- Peter preaches that Christ is the Messiah and that He rose from the dead. About three thousand people are baptized.

When the time for Pentecost was fulfilled, the were all in one place together. And suddenly there came from the sky a noise like a strong driving wind, and it filled the entire house in which they were. Then there appeared to them tongues as of fire, which parted and came to rest on each one of them. And they were all filled with the holy Spirit and began to speak in different tongues, as the Spirit enabled them to proclaim.

Now there were devout Jews from every nation under heaven staying in Jerusalem... they were confused because each one heard them speaking in his own language. They were astounded, and in amazement they asked, "Are not all these people who are speaking Galileans? Then how does each of us hear them in his own native language. (Acts 2:1–8)

God raised this Jesus; of this we are all witnesses. Exalted at the right hand of God, he received the promise of the holy Spirit from the Father and poured it forth, as you [both] see and hear. (Acts 2:32–33)

Therefore let the whole house of Israel know for certain that God has made him both Lord and Messiah, this Jesus whom you crucified." (Acts 2:36)

Lectio Divina | PRAYING WITH SCRIPTURE

God's love is poured into our hearts by the Holy Spirit (Romans 5:5). Ask this question in prayer: "Jesus, You promised to send the Holy Spirit after returning to the Father. How can I be more aware to the promptings of the Holy Spirit in my life?" What do you hear Him saying to you?

VIRTUE | CHARITY

Enables one to love as God Himself loves, to love God
above all things and one's neighbor as oneself

Ways to Cultivate This Virtue

- Volunteer to help someone in their yard or house.
- Look for ways to help the sick, hungry, troubled.
- Visit the Blessed Sacrament.
- Praise God and tell Him you love Him.

I'M PRAYING THIS DECADE FOR: _____

- Mary longs to see her Son.
- She "falls asleep" in peace and is laid to rest.
- Mary is taken up, body and soul, into heaven and is received joyously.
- The Apostles find her tomb empty.

"Arise, my beloved, my beautiful one, and come!...You are all-beautiful, my beloved, and there is no blemish in you." (Song of Songs 2:10, 4:7)

The daughter of the king is clothed with splendor, her robes embroidered with pearls set in gold. She is led to the king with her maiden companions. They are escorted amid gladness and joy; they pass within the palace of the king. (Psalm 45:14–16)

Then God's temple in heaven was opened, and the ark of his covenant could be seen in the temple. A great sign appeared in the sky, a woman clothed with the sun. (Revelation 12:1)

Lectio Divina | PRAYING WITH SCRIPTURE

Ask this question in prayer: "Jesus, Your Mother is pure in body and soul and was taken up to heaven. Show me how I can be more pure in body and soul so as to see You." What do you hear Him saying to you?

VIRTUE | MAGNANIMITY

Seeking with confidence to do great things in God; literally "having a large soul"

Ways to Cultivate This Virtue

- Compliment someone else when you want to be recognized.
- Acknowledge the good in others when it is difficult.
- Ask God to help you do great things for Him.
- Always try to do more for others.

I'M PRAYING THIS DECADE FOR: _____

- Jesus crowns Mary Queen of Heaven and earth.
- Mary is enthroned beside Jesus.
- Mary is seen crowned with twelve stars.
- Those in heaven and on earth praise Mary.
- Mary intercedes for us with her Son.

A great sign appeared in the sky, a woman clothed with the sun, with the moon under her feet, and on her head a crown of twelve stars… She gave birth to a son, a male child, destined to rule all the nations with an iron rod. (Revelation 12:1,5)

And Mary said: "My soul proclaims the greatness of the LORD;
 my spirit rejoices in God my savior.
For he has looked upon his handmaid's lowliness;
 behold, from now on will all ages call me blessed.
The Almighty has done great things for me,
 and holy is His name." (Luke 1:46-48)

Lectio Divina | PRAYING WITH SCRIPTURE

We experience the joy of living in goodness and truth. Ask Jesus to show you one virtue you need to cultivate to be more fully alive. What do you hear Him saying to you?

"The glory of God is the human being fully alive; the life of man consists in beholding God." —St. Irenaeus

VIRTUE | LOYALTY

Accepting the bonds implicit in relationships;
defending virtues upheld by Church, family, and country

Ways to Cultivate This Virtue

- Speak positively about your family and friends.
- Stand up for someone if he/she is being bullied.
- Make your actions correspond to your words and promises.
- Seek to do your best to help others.

Blessed Fra Angelico
(1400-1455)

The majority of the artwork in this book is the work of the early Renaissance painter known as Blessed Fra Angelico (Italian for "Angelic Brother"). He was born in Florence, Italy, where he also entered the Order of Preachers (the Dominicans) and was known in religion as Giovanni da Fiesole.

Fra Angelico preached eloquently by his paintings, using his brush to make visible the mysteries of God which he contemplated. His frescoes, altarpieces, and miniatures adorn the walls of the Dominican priory of San Marco in Florence and are spread throughout Italy. Pope Eugene IV commissioned him to decorate various chapels in Rome and the Vatican.

His work is notable for the rich use of color and the serenity of the figures. It is said that the heavenly qualities of his work derive from the help of the angels, as depicted in the painting by Paul-Hippolyte Flandrin on the opposite page. He was renowned for his holiness and for his excellence as an artist, being called beato ("blessed") and angelico ("angelic") not long after his death on account of his virtues.

John Paul II gave Blessed Fra Angelico special attention in his *Letter to Artists* (1999):

> *"Every genuine artistic intuition goes beyond what the senses perceive and, reaching beneath reality's surface, strives to interpret its hidden mystery. The intuition itself springs from the depths of the human soul...[T]he dazzling perfection of the beauty glimpsed in the ardour of the creative moment: what [artists] manage to express in their painting, their sculpting, their creating is no more than a glimmer of the splendour which flared for a moment before the eyes of their spirit...*
>
> *The knowledge conferred by faith...presupposes a personal encounter with God in Jesus Christ. Yet this knowledge too can be enriched by artistic intuition. An eloquent example of aesthetic contemplation sublimated in faith are, for example, the works of Fra Angelico."*

Blessed Fra Angelico's feast day is February 18. He is the patron saint of artists.

References

Cover Image: *Virgin and Child* (oil on panel), Orley, Bernard van (c.1488-1541) / Prado, Madrid, Spain / Bridgeman Images

Page 7: *The Elect* (chromolitho), French School, (19th century) / Private Collection / © Look and Learn / Bridgeman Images

Page 12: *The Annunciation*, 1425-8 (tempera on wood), Angelico, Fra (Guido di Pietro) (c.1387-1455) / Prado, Madrid, Spain / Bridgeman Images

Page 14: *Visitation*, from the predella of the Annunciation Alterpiece, c.1430-32 (tempera & gold on panel), Angelico, Fra (Guido di Pietro) (c.1387-1455) / Prado, Madrid, Spain / Bridgeman Images

Page 16: *The Nativity*, c.1425-30 (tempera on poplar panel), Angelico, Fra (Guido di Pietro) (c.1387-1455) / Minneapolis Institute of Arts, MN, USA / Bequest of Miss Tessie Jones in memory of Herschel V. Jones / Bridgeman Images

Page 18: *Presentation of Jesus at the Temple*, by Giovanni da Fiesole, known as Fra Angelico (ca 1400-1455), fresco. Tenth cell, Convent of St Mark's, Florence / De Agostini Picture Library / Bridgeman Images

Page 20: *Maesta*: *Christ Among the Doctors*, 1308-11, Duccio di Buoninsegna, (c.1278-1318) / Museo dell'Opera del Duomo, Siena, Italy / Wikimedia Commons / Public Domain

Page 24: *Baptism of Christ* (Battesimo di Cristo), by Giotto, 1303-1305, 14th century (fresco), Giotto di Bondone (c.1266-1337) / Scrovegni (Arena) Chapel, Padua, Italy / Mondadori Portfolio/Archivio Antonio Quattrone/ Antonio Quattrones / Bridgeman Images

Page 26: *Scenes from the Life of Christ*, panels one and two from the Silver Treasury of Santissima Annunziata, c.1450-53 (tempera on panel), Angelico, Fra (c.1387-1455) & Baldovinetti, Alesso (1425-99) / Museo di San Marco, Florence, Italy / Bridgeman Images

Page 28: *The Sermon on the Mount*, 1442 (fresco), Angelico, Fra (Guido di Pietro) (c.1387-1455) / Museo di San Marco, Florence, Italy / Bridgeman Images

Page 30: *Transfiguration*, 1438-1450, by Giovanni da Fiesole, known as Fra Angelico (ca 1400-1455), fresco, Detail, Convent of San Marco, Florence, Italy / De Agostini Picture Library / G. Nimatallah / Bridgeman Images

Page 32: *The Last Supper*, 1442 (fresco), Angelico, Fra (Guido di Pietro) (c.1387-1455) / Museo di San Marco, Florence, Italy / Bridgeman Images

Page 36: *The Agony in the Garden*, detail from panel three of the Silver Treasury of Santissima Annunziata, c.1450-53 (tempera on panel), Angelico, Fra (Guido di Pietro) (c.1387-1455) (and workshop) / Museo di San Marco, Florence, Italy / Bridgeman Images

Page 38: *Inset depicting the flogging of Jesus*, panel from the Armadio degli Argenti (Silver Chest) with life of Jesus, 1451-1453, by Giovanni da Fiesole known as Fra Angelico (1400-ca 1455), tempera on wood / De Agostini Picture Library / G. Nimatallah / Bridgeman Images

Page 40: *Christ Mocked in the Presence of the Virgin and Saint Dominic* (fresco), Angelico, Fra (c.1387-1455) (school of) / Church of San Marco, Florence, Italy / Alinari / Bridgeman Images

Page 42: *Christ Carrying The Cross*, c.1438-45 (fresco), Angelico, Fra (Guido di Pietro) (c.1387-1455) / Museo di San Marco, Florence, Italy / Bridgeman Images

Page 44: *Crucifixion with Saints*, by Giovanni da Fiesole, known as Fra Angelico (ca 1400-1455), fresco. Chapter house of the Convent of San Marco, Florence. / De Agostini Picture Library / Bridgeman Images

Page 48: *The Resurrection of Christ and the Pious Women at the Sepulchre*, 1442 (fresco), Angelico, Fra (Guido di Pietro) (c.1387-1455) / Museo di San Marco, Florence, Italy / Bridgeman Images

Page 50: *The Ascension*, c.1305 (fresco), Giotto di Bondone (c.1266-1337) / Scrovegni (Arena) Chapel, Padua, Italy / Bridgeman Images

Page 52: *Pentecost*, c.1366-68 (fresco), Andrea di Bonaiuto (Andrea da Firenze) (fl.1342-77) (after) / Santa Maria Novella, Florence, Italy / Bridgeman Images

Page 54: *The Dormition and the Assumption of the Virgin*, c.1430 (gold & tempera on panel), Angelico, Fra (Guido di Pietro) (c.1387-1455) / Isabella Stewart Gardner Museum, Boston, MA / Bridgeman Images

Page 56: *The Coronation of the Virgin*, c.1440 (tempera on panel), Angelico, Fra (Guido di Pietro) (c.1387-1455) / Galleria degli Uffizi, Florence, Tuscany, Italy / Bridgeman Images

References

Page 58: **Portrait of Fra Angelico**, Portrait of Fra Angelico, by Luca Signorelli, detail of Deeds of the Antichrist fresco (c.1501) in Orvieto Cathedral . Image courtesy of Web Gallery of Art, Wikimedia Commons, Public Domain

Page 59: **Fra Angelico Visited by the Angels**, Paul-Hippolyte Flandrin 1894, oil on canvas, Musée des Beaux-Arts de Rouen, Wikimedia Commons / Public Domain

Quote References

St. Bernadette Soubirous, as quoted in Don Sharkey, *The Woman Shall Conquer: The Story of the Blessed Virgin in the Modern World* (Milwaukee: Bruce Publishing Company, 1952), 56

St. Pope John XXIII, as quoted in Fr. Patrick Peyton, *All For Her* (Hollywood, California: Family Theater Productions, 1973), 189

Venerable Fulton J. Sheen, *The World's First Love: Mary, Mother of God* (San Francisco, California: Ignatius Press, 1996), 214-215

Blessed Michael Sopocko, *The Mercy of God in His Works: Vol. IV*, trans. R. Batchelor (Hereford: Marian Apostolate, 1972), 86

St. Padre Pio, as quoted in Liz Kelly, *The Rosary: A Path to Prayer* (Chicago, Illinois: Loyola Press, 2004), 86

Servant of God (Fr.) Joseph Kentenich, *Mary, Our Mother and Educator: An Applied Mariology*, trans. Johnathan Niehaus (Waukesha, Wisconsin: Shoenstatt Sisters, 1987), 11

Blessed Pope Pius IX, as quoted in Msgr. Joseph A. Cirrincione & Thomas A. Nelson, *The Rosary and the Crisis of Faith* (Rockford, Illinois: TAN Books, 1986), 35

Servant of God (Fr.) Patrick Peyton, in *Mary, the Pope, and the American Apostle of the Family Rosary*, by Fr. Willy Raymond, CSC in Behold Your Mother: Priests Speak about Mary. (ed.). Stephen J. Rossetti (Notre Dame, Indiana: Ave Maria Press, 2007), 53

Venerable Fulton J. Sheen, *The World's First Love: Mary, Mother of God* (San Francisco, California: Ignatius Press, 1996), 210

Blessed Pope Pius IV, as quoted in Don Sharkey, *The Woman Shall Conquer: The Story of the Blessed Virgin in the Modern World* (Milwaukee: Bruce Publishing Company, 1952), 246 Pope Leo XIII, *Fidentem piumque animum* (September 20, 1896), 5

Servant of God (Fr.) Dolindo Ruotolo, *Meditations on the Holy Rosary of Mary*, trans. Giovanna Invitti Ellis (Napoli, Italy, 2006), 4

Servant of God Pope John Paul I, as quoted in *Humilitas*, English edition, Vol. XXIII, No. 4, December 2012, ed. Ray and Lauretta Seabeck, Mother Teresa OCD, trans. Lori Pieper (Missionary Servants of Pope John Paul I, Beaverton, Oregon

Servant of God, (Fr.) Patrick Peyton, as quoted in Jeanne Gosselin Arnold, *A Man of Faith: Father Patrick Peyton, CSC* (Hollywood, California: Family Theater, Inc., 1983), 250

Venerable Fulton J. Sheen, *The World's First Love: Mary, Mother of God* (San Francisco, California: Ignatius Press, 1996), 209

Blessed Barolo Longo, as quoted in *St. Joun Paul II, Rosarium Virginis Mariae*, 15

Venerable Pope Pius XII, as quoted in Jeanne Gosselin Arnold, *A Man of Faith: Father Patrick Peyton, CSC* (Hollywood, California: Family Theater, Inc., 1983), 99.

St. Josemaría Escrivá, *The Way*, no. 558, p. 117

Blessed Bartolo Longo, as quoted in Ann M. Brown, *Apostle of the Rosary: Blessed Bartolo Longo* (New Hope, Kentucky: New Hope Publications, 2004), 43

Pope Francis, *Address at the Vigil of Pentecost with the Ecclesial Movements*, (May 18, 2013)

This Shield is an emblem of the Order of Preachers, recalling the black and white habit worn by Saint Dominic and by his sons and daughters in the Order.

Where did the Rosary come from?

The prayers spring from Scripture. Jesus Himself taught us the Our Father (Matthew 6:9–13, Luke 11:2–4). The Hail Mary comprises the angel Gabriel's greeting to Mary (Luke 1:28), her cousin Elizabeth's words of praise (Luke 1:42) and a petition for Mary's help that developed from popular devotion and received its final form after the Council of Trent (1545-63). The Glory Be draws upon St. Paul's frequent expressions of giving glory to God (e.g. Romans 11:36, Galatians 1:5, Ephesians 3:21) and has existed in the form we know it since the seventh century.

These prayers began to be gathered and prayed in association with various mysteries of Christ's life around the eleventh and twelfth centuries. Religious and others who had not learned to read would pray the Hail Mary 150 times, once for each of the 150 Psalms. This gradually developed into three sets of five mysteries, each mystery meditated upon during the course of ten Hail Marys. In his 2002 letter on the rosary, *Rosarium Virginis Mariae*, St. Pope John Paul II recommended an additional set of five mysteries, the Luminous Mysteries, to join the traditional Joyful, Sorrowful, and Glorious.

The rosary is closely associated with the Dominican Order. It developed at the historical moment when St. Dominic was founding his Order of Friars to preach the truth about Christ under Mary's protection. St. Dominic himself is said always to have begun his own preaching with a Hail Mary, and his spiritual sons, particularly Bl. Alan de la Roche, St. Louis de Montfort, and St. Pius V promoted the devotion among the faithful. The Dominican habit includes a fifteen-decade rosary hung from the cincture on one's left side.

The name "rosary" originates in the description of the Bride in the Song of Songs as a "rose of Sharon, a lily of the valleys" (Song 2:1). When we pray the rosary, we offer the prayers as a bouquet or crown of roses to our beloved Mother.

[Much of this history is drawn from the Manual for Marian Devotion (Tan Books, 2016).]

Dominican Sisters *of* Mary
Mother *of the* Eucharist